Sudden Champion

The Sarah Hughes Story

Amanda + Elizabeth,
I hope someday
you'll both be `champions'!
Richard Krawiec
1/14/05

Sudden Champion
The Sarah Hughes Story

Richard Krawiec

Avisson Press, Inc.
Greensboro

ISBN 1-888105-53-4
First edition
Printed in the USA

Publisher's Cataloging-in-Publication
(Provided by Quality Books, Inc.)

Krawiec, Richard
  Sudden champion : the Sarah Hughes story / Richard Krawiec. —
1st ed.
    p. cm. — (Avisson young adult series)
    Includes index.
    ISBN 1-888105-53-4

  1. Hughes, Sarah, 1985- — Juvenile literature.
2. Skaters—United States—Biography—Juvenile literature.
3. Women skaters—United States—Biography—Juvenile literature.
[1. Hughes, Sarah, 1985- 2. Ice skaters. 3. Women—Biography.]
I. Title. II. Series.
GV850.H87K73 2002   796.91'092
                         QB102-701992

Library of Congress Control Number: 2002113929

Photo credits: All photos including cover courtesy of AP/Wide World Photos.

Dedication

To every child who has a dream and is
willing to work hard for it.

— R.K

Contents

Chapter 1

From the center of the ice rink, the skater doesn't really see the thousands of people peering intently with hushed breath, waiting for the routine to begin. But the skater can feel them there, shapes and forms, pulses of energy all focused on her.

When she glided out to begin her long program at the 2002 Olympic Winter Games in Salt Lake City, Sarah Hughes felt that energy.

It was a bit subdued, perhaps. Polite. As she herself said afterwards, "A lot of people had already counted me out." She was, after all, not a real name in the sport; her noted accomplishments were few. And, she was only sicteen years old.

There were other reasons not to be excited about Sarah Hughes. She had skated disappointingly the previous month, at the United States National Championships in Los Angeles, and finished third.

Entering the Olympics, it seemed like the American followers of women's figure skating had turned against Hughes, focusing their attention on Sasha Cohen as the new teenaged darling, the skater with the best chance of beating everyone's odds-on favorite, the veteran Michelle Kwan. Sasha Cohen had charmed the international skating world. She could spin like a dervish, skate with energy and flare. She was a fiery dynamo on the ice, flashy, dramatic, and had the impish good looks of a naughty princess.

Even if Hughes could beat out Cohen, there was still Kwan, who despite her recent uneven performances, was the reigning Queen of the Ice Skating World, with a larger collection of gold medals than those of Cohen and Hughes combined. Michelle Kwan, of course, skated with a grace and flow that some claimed made her skating the most beautiful the world had ever seen. Going into the games, she was clearly the most popular female skater in the world.

Compared to Cohen's risqué allure, and Kwan's

feminine delicacy and grace, Hughes, with her long, drawn face and overbite, her five-foot-four-and-a-half inch frame, huge by skating standards, might appear to be the ugly duckling of American figure skating. She had her fans and supporters, to be sure. But the *cognoscenti*, the knowledgeable insiders, had already relegated her to the second tier of performers, behind Kwan, Cohen, and the muscular Russian champion, Irina Slutskaya, who had beaten Kwan three times in the six months leading up to the Olympics.

The dismissive judgment of the critics seemed justified when Sarah Hughes finished fourth in the short program at the Olympics, a full 1.5 points behind Michelle Kwan.

At that point, even Hughes had her doubts, later telling Selena Roberts of the *New York Times*, "I didn't think it possible (to win the gold), being fourth."

No skater had ever moved up from fourth in the short program to win an Olympic gold. Perhaps Sarah Hughes had an outside chance at a bronze, but with Kwan being so far ahead, and Slutskaya, noted for her ability to leap high into the air and nail difficult triple-triples, also ahead of her (not to mention the crowd-pleaser Cohen, who had spoken earlier of being the first woman skater to attempt a quadruple combination), no one really gave Hughes a serious chance.

But then the odds against Sarah Hughes grew even worse.

The draw to determine the skating order slotted Hughes fourth from last, right before the three skaters ranked above her. This put her at a considerable disadvantage. Would the judges, who are notorious for underscoring early skaters, hold back on scoring Hughes too highly because the acknowledged top three skaters in the program were scheduled to follow her?

As if that weren't enough, like a final nail in the coffin of her expectations, there was the problem with the Russians.

Earlier in the Olympics, there had been a public uproar over the awarding of the gold medal in pairs skating to the Russian couple Elena Berezhnaya and Anton Sikharulidze. Canada's Jamie Sale and David Pelletier had seemed to the crowd, and many skating experts, to win the event. An analysis of the video showed that the audience reaction was correct. The Russians had made multiple mistakes, including stumbling when landing a routine jump. The Canadian pair had skated flawlessly.

The International Skating Union had conducted a hurried investigation. There were accusations that pressure had been brought to bear on the judges, back room deals made. Some fellow judges signed affidavits that claimed the French judge buckled under pressure and scored the Russians higher than she would have normally. The scores of the back-up judges validated this argument.

Another investigation by the International Olympic Union concluded that the French judge, Marie Reine Le Gaugne, had been improperly pressured to vote for the Russian team pair. In return, the Russians would vote for the French ice dancers in a later competition.

Eager to cover up the scandal, the International Olympic Committee withdrew Gagne's score and substituted the score of the replacement judge, who had awarded first place to the Canadians. The IOC awarded a second set of gold medals to the Canadian pairs skaters, but allowed the Russians to keep theirs.

The Russians grumbled. Then they complained that their hockey team lost because their game against Canada was officiated too closely. Finally, when a Russian cross-country skier was disqualified from medal contention after a blood test showed traces of drugs, the Russian contingent threatened to remove all their athletes from the games.

On the evening before the women's figure skating final, the entire Russian contingent, mired in fifth place in the medals race, was threatening to go home.

As Robert Sullivan wrote in *Time magazine online*, many believed this was purposely done to influence the judges in favor of the Russian skater, Irina Slutskaya. "Pressures bearing upon the ultimate decision in ladies figure skating included not only hidebound judging traditions and lingering Cold War resentment, but also Russia's heretofore lousy performance at this Olympics," Sullivan wrote.

With all this hullabaloo, with the tough and seasoned competition, no one gave Sarah Hughes much of a chance at a medal. Which, surprisingly, was all right with Sarah. "There was no pressure on me to win. I skated for pure enjoyment. That's how

I wanted my Olympic moment to be," she later told the *New York Times*.

Sarah Hughes looked forward to skating, not to win a medal, but simply to have fun. Or so she said. But...but...Sarah and her coach, Robin Wagner, knew there was more to it. Once on the ice, Sarah was like a thoroughbred racehorse. There was no way she was willing to settle for less than the best.

"I really believe that in her competitive heart," Wagner told the *New York Times*, "she knew there was a way to win. And that's what makes a champion."

Everyone who had already counted Sarah Hughes out had made one very big mistake. They had underestimated Sarah's heart, her competitive drive, her ebullient will to succeed.

Never in her life had Sarah Hughes given up without a fight. Anyone who thought Sarah would be content to skate for fun, maybe settle for a bronze medal, didn't know anything about the type of person Sarah was, or where she had come from. As Wagner pointed out, "The fire inside her is something you're born with . . ."

Chapter 2

As many people know, hockey isn't so much a sport in Canada as it is a religion. People worship hockey players and teams. Children grow up dreaming of playing for the fabled Montreal Canadians or Toronto Maple Leafs.

Because of Canada's long, cold winters, not just the lakes and ponds, but even the rivers freeze into hard, smooth surfaces ideal for skating. In winter, everywhere you go in that country you see children skating for hours on end. The air resounds with the deep, sharp slap of wooden sticks hitting against hard rubber pucks. Gleeful voices keen through the cold, boys screaming as their team scores a goal.

John Hughes, who would become the father of another, more famous paragon of the ice, was no different than any other Canadian boy. He grew up in Scarborough, Canada, with the same dream as all his friends –- the dream of being a professional hockey player. But what set John apart from many of his friends was the dedication he brought to his attempt to achieve that dream.

From a young age, John spent every moment he could on the ice, working on his skating, struggling to improve his game. He seemed preternaturally determined, even for a Canadian boy; one of those rare children able to focus on a long-term goal and work towards it year after year.

For Hughes, all the effort, all the hard work, seemed to pay off when he enrolled at Cornell University. Cornell was not only a prestigious Ivy League school, it was also known for having one of the top collegiate hockey programs in the United States.

John Hughes not only made the hockey team, but in 1969 he was named captain. In that 1969-1970 season, the Cornell hockey team, due in no small part to John Hughes' determination and leadership, won the national college championship.

Hughes had earned himself a tryout with the

Toronto Maple Leafs. It seemed as if his childhood dream would come true.

But the world of professional hockey is quite a step up from the world of college hockey. Many great college players simply can't make the leap to that higher level. John Hughes, at Cornell, had taken his talent as far as he could. His hockey dreams would end with his college career.

When things didn't work out with the Maple Leafs, Hughes returned to Cornell to attend law school. He applied himself to his law studies with the same diligence and dedication he had brought to hockey.

In due time he met, wooed, and married Amy Pasternack, who had graduated from Wheaton College in 1967. Amy was a lively, energetic young woman, a woman also known for her ability to focus on a goal and persevere until she had accomplished it. It was a good match – two high achievers, two people who didn't understand the word 'quit'.

John built a successful career for himself as a lawyer. He was so successful, in fact, that he and Amy were able to settle down and raise a family in King's Point, a wealthy suburb on Long Island.

King's Point is one of nine villages on Long Island's north shore. The villages combine to form the area known as Great Neck.

Great Neck was used to fame and notoriety. It had long been a favored haunt of celebrities. In the early part of the Twentieth Century, celebrities like the comedian Groucho Marx, and writer George S. Kaufman, had gone to Great Neck to party at the homes of the wealthy elite. F. Scott Fitzgerald set his "jazz age" novel, *The Great Gatsby*, in a fictionalized version of Great Neck.

It's the type of place where the most common car seems to be a Mercedes Benz, and even the thrift shops feature items with designer labels. The school Sarah Hughes was destined to attend, Great Neck North High School, was the same school that graduated director Francis Ford Coppola and legendary comedian Andy Kaufman.

John and Amy Hughes, two people who were themselves very competitive, driven to excel, were well suited to the environment. The Hughes were not the sort of people who would move to some rural backwater, willing to settle for being the big frogs in a small pond. They wanted to achieve, and be measured, against the best.

It was into this environment that Sarah Hughes was born on May 2, 1985 in Manhasset, New York.

By the time Sarah arrived, her parents already had three children: Rebecca, who was five years old; David, who was three; and Matthew, who was one. Sarah was certainly loved, fawned over as all babies are, but she was the fourth child in a family that would soon expand to include six children. As every parent knows, there are only so many minutes in the day, only so much attention to go around.

There were three other children ahead of baby Sarah; three children who already had years of experience in clambering for their parents' attention.

In a way, being the fourth child, Sarah's experience was similar to that of a second child— only doubled. With an older sister and two older brothers ahead of her in the pecking order, Sarah had to play not second, but fourth fiddle. She might very well be ignored, pushed into the background. Unless she was willing to push herself to the forefront of her parents' attention.

As loving and attentive as her parents were, there may have been times when Sarah felt overlooked. By the time she was three, her mother was getting ready to give birth to another child, another baby girl, Emily. Another baby in need of her parents' love and attention.

Sarah's early desire for attention proved to be an important factor in her development as a skater. As she later told *Cleveland.com*, "I enjoy being the center of attention." But what could a young child do when surrounded by so much competition?

What crystallized things for Sarah, gave her a focus, was the day her father installed an ice rink in the back yard. The rink was for everyone to use, to be sure. But her brothers harbored their own hockey dreams, and John Hughes, in his deepest heart, was hoping, like any father would, that the rink might help one of them achieve John's old dream of becoming a professional player.

But as Sarah later told the *Today Show*'s Katie Couric, she did not want to be excluded. "We all used to go skating together and my brothers played hockey. I just wanted to do whatever they did." Sarah, at three, had no desire to be left out. She insisted on her share of the ice.

When it became apparent the backyard rink was too small for David and Matthew to practice their hockey on, Sarah's mother decided to bring the boys to the Parkwood Ice Skating Rink in Great Neck.

Sarah, not wanting to be left out, got her coat on and waited for them at the door.

The first time they visited the rink, Sarah bolted onto the ice before anyone else was ready. Amy, who was nearing the end of her pregnancy with Emily, couldn't move fast enough to stop her three-year-old daughter. So the next time they visited the rink, her mother decided to tie Sarah's skates last, thinking that would keep her daughter waiting patiently on the bench.

Sarah, even then, was so determined not to be left behind, she figured out how to tie her skates on her own, and headed for center ice.

Not willing to merely cede attention to her older siblings, Sarah took to skating with a vengeance. She exhibited the same determination to succeed that had been primary characteristics of both her parents' personalities. Sarah was determined to prove she was just as good, just as worthy of their attention, as everyone else.

Although she may have been driven initially by her desire for attention, Sarah soon realized she loved skating. Loved everything about it. The feeling of speed and grace as she zipped around the ice; the cute costumes and make-up; the applause, the attention from people who watched her; the inner joy that came from recognizing she could do this thing, this skating, better than anyone around her.

It didn't take long for her parents to realize Sarah's drive to excel was exceptional. Noted father John, "We didn't direct her toward skating. If I'd directed her anywhere, it would have been to hockey." Combining the determination of her father, the joy and ebullience of her mother, Sarah, even at three years of age, had a special aura about her when she was on the ice.

She had certainly found a way to get her parents' attention. John and Amy signed their daughter up for lessons at the Parkwood Ice Skating Rink. Sarah was the youngest skater in her group; all the other children were at least four or five years old.

In a move that proved prescient, John and Amy also enrolled Sarah in ballet classes, to help her develop grace and form.

By the time she was six, her mother was ready to give birth once more. One more baby coming into the Hughes' world, an additional child needing love and attention. It was at this point in time that Sarah took her first glide into the public eye. She skated in an exhibition with Peggy Fleming. Sarah idolized Fleming, who had won a gold medal at the 1968 Olympics, and just to be on the same ice with her hero was thrilling.

As if that weren't enough of a thrill, the crowd applauded enthusiastically for Sarah. And Fleming praised the little girl as being talented beyond her years.

Sarah Hughes was hooked. She had found a place where she could do something she loved more than anything else in the world, and she could get all the attention and approval she needed — at the center of a skating rink.

Sarah dedicated herself to skating even more intensely. In another two years, when she was eight, Sarah earned a spot on a skating troupe heading for a tour of France. The traveling program featured Olympic skaters Surya Bonaly and Alexander Zhulin. Hughes told *People* magazine this experience really gave her a focus for her talents. "When I saw the Olympic skaters, I thought, 'I want to do that.' It gave me something to aspire to."

For her father, this tour was amazing. He sat in rink after rink, surrounded by thousands of people, while, on the ice, his daughter skated without showing the least concern about being the center of so many people's attention.

"That's when I felt this was something she was going to do," John Hughes later told *U.S. Figure Skating Online*.

♟

By age nine, Sarah was skating regularly at Madison Square Garden, doing short programs between periods of the New York Rangers hockey games.

Most children would be intimidated by having to skate in front of such large, raucous crowds. Not Sarah, though. The noise of the large crowds enthralled her.

It was in the following year, the year she turned ten, that Sarah's true destiny became set. But it might never have happened if not for a decision her parents had made when Sarah was only three.

Chapter 4

In recent times, the Russian skaters have been the dominant influence in the international ice skating scene, especially the male dancers and pairs skaters. Skaters from all over the world have emulated the Russian mixture of power skating and artistic grace.

Before the breakup of the former Soviet Union, it wasn't unusual for the elementary school day to run from 8:30 to 12:30. This left plenty of time for practice. Like Canada, many parts of Russia are very cold, so lakes and ponds and rivers freeze hard, providing ample opportunity for children to develop their skills.

A typical child chosen for training might well

attend practice sessions both before and after school. It was not unusual for a child who was identified early as a potential athlete to skate five times a week, while also working on choreography twice a week, and spending three days exercising and studying dance. In summertime, the children would leave home for intensive skating camps directed by expert trainers

But even after other countries began to drill their skaters in technique and form, following the Russian model, the Russians still continued to skate in a way that commanded attention at most international competitions.

What gave the Russians their edge was not just their intensive skate training program, but their dance heritage. Russian skaters don't do all their work on the ice. They enroll in classical dance classes, where they receive training that is just as rigorous as the training they receive in ice-skating. Year after year Russian skaters would receive equal training in dance studios and ice rinks.

There was a slight downside, however, to the Russian emphasis on dance training. In classical ballet, dance solos are certainly common. But, in most cases, a dancer can express more ideas with a partner, than by dancing alone. This school of thought extended from the stage to the ice, where Russian skaters excelled in pairs dancing. The Russian skating program placed far less emphasis on training individuals to dance solo routines. It wasn't until Russian skaters and coaches began to leave the country that the Russian style began to influence singles skaters.

Since the end of the cold war, many Russian dancers and coaches have immigrated to the countries in Europe and the United States, bringing with them the artistic techniques they learned in their homeland. In recent years, American skaters have begun to incorporate dance training as an essential part of their skate training. They have learned the lesson of the Russians, and it shows in the medals count at international skating events. A background in classical choreography matters.

Americans are now garnering a larger and larger share of gold, silver, and bronze medals on the world stage. Many American skaters, including Sarah Hughes' rivals, Michelle Kwan and Sasha Cohen, had extensive training in classical dance. Such training is now considered to be a necessity if one is to compete as a skater against the world's best.

�҉

Sarah Hughes was to prove no exception to this trend. When she was three, her parents took her to the Great Neck School of Dance. Sarah was signed up to be tutored by former ballerina Roberta Senn.

"Sarah always had the ability to put it together," Senn told *Newsday*. "Some people can learn all the moves, all the extensions and the positions, but can't put it together in a dance."

But Sarah could.

To Senn, Sarah wasn't merely an ice skater trying to develop grace. She was a star pupil, a girl who had the talent to pursue a professional dance career.

For the next eleven years, Senn worked with Sarah. She taught the girl how to do arabesques, double piques, triple pirouettes. Sarah excelled at them all, performing with a grace often hoped for, but rarely seen, in young children. As *Newsday* reported, "To a dance teacher, Hughes was one of the finds of a lifetime."

But it wasn't to be.

"This was a child who was never, ever interested in becoming a ballet dancer," Senn noted sadly as she watched a video of her former pupil on the dance floor. "She wanted to be a skater. Never wavered. I wanted her to be a ballet dancer. I thought she could be very good."

For eleven years, Roberta Senn taught Sarah about grace and movement. Then it was time for Sarah to move forward in dance, to make the leap to the next level. It was time for Sarah to learn the difficult maneuver known as *en Pointe*; dancing on her toes.

The Hughes family decided it was too dangerous. Sarah might hurt her feet. And that might hurt her skating. At the age of fourteen, Sarah ended her formal dance training.

♛

But the lessons learned wouldn't go for naught. The example of the powerful and graceful Russians would be fully utilized. The lessons begun when Sarah was three, began to be incorporated into her skating when she was ten. That was the year the Hughes family hired a 'failed' skater, a woman who had never trained a champion, to be Sarah's choreographer.

Chapter 5

The decision John and Amy Hughes made for their daughter in 1995 turned out to be the most crucial one of Sarah's career. They hired Robin Wagner to be Sarah's choreographer. By 1998, Wagner had moved into the role of fulltime coach.

But in 1995, when Robin was hired to be Sarah's choreographer, marked the first time a trained professional, someone who knew about skating competitions, took control of Sarah's development. It's interesting to note that the Hughes' choice was to hire someone to emphasize choreography, presentation. They weren't strictly looking for an ice skating coach.

Although Roberta Senn would soon lose her

star pupil, Sarah was in the hands of someone who valued and appreciated all that Senn had done.

At first glance, it seemed a curious move for the Hughes to hire Robin Wagner. Although Robin had been a skater two and a half decades earlier, competing at the 1974 and 1975 U.S. Nationals Championship, she had never won a medal.

It is common in the skating world for former champions to train future champions. Although, not every medalled skater has a former champion as a trainer. But conventional wisdom holds that, if you're not going to hire a former champion, you must hire one of the big name coaches who have developed a reputation for cranking out champion-caliber skaters. Someone like Michelle Kwan's first coach, Frank Carroll, who had a record of success dating back to 1977, when he handled World Champion Linda Frattiane.

Wagner was neither a former champion, nor a 'big name' coach. She had never coached a single student to the World Championships.

But she was someone the Hughes felt comfortable having around the house. Being a family that believed in the value of education, they appreciated the fact that Wagner, who had graduated from Barnard College in New York, was intelligent and well rounded. Wagner enjoyed reading, liked to attend plays, operas, and dance performances. There were a lot of things she could discuss besides skating. The Hughes found this an important quality in a coach, because they didn't want Sarah to become nothing more than a skating machine.

Both Wagner and the Hughes family agreed on how best to handle the young skater. They felt it imperative that Sarah stay in school, not drop out and take all her classes with tutors. They wanted their daughter to have the social experience that comes from having classmates. They wanted Sarah to have as normal a life as possible, and not turn out so obsessively focused on skating that there would be nothing else she lived for.

The plan seemed to succeed. Sarah grew into, if not exactly a home girl someone who has many of the trappings of normalcy, if there is such a thing as a normal teen. Sarah developed an early talent for music and played the violin in the school orchestra.

She likes nothing better than to open the oven at home and bake cookies for her two older brothers. She is a television fan listing such shows as *7th Heaven, Will and Grace,* and *Seinfield* as favorites. She also occasionally enjoys pigging out on Japanese or Italian food.

This desire for normalcy, this desire to keep Sarah grounded, also showed up in the practice routine Wagner developed.

Initially Wagner worked with Sarah at the Parkwood Ice Rink, where Sarah had gone through five levels of training. Soon, however, it became clear to Hughes that if her pupil were to make a serious push for a skating career, she would have to move to a different practice site. There was simply not enough ice time available at the Parkwood Ice Rink to develop a rigorous training schedule. And when Sarah could get on the ice, it was often too crowded.

Wagner found an excellent alternative, an ice skating complex in Hackensack, New Jersey.

The Ice House was built in response to the growing number of youth hockey leagues in the Hackensack area. With four full-sized rinks, it was one of the finest facilities on the East Coast. Since most young hockey players attend public school during the day, hockey practices are usually held at night, or early in the morning.

Sarah's middle school was willing to work around her schedule, supplementing classwork with tutoring sessions. It was arranged for Sarah to attend her school for only a couple of hours each day. This meant there would be plenty of ice time available during the day for her to practice her figure skating.

Because the Ice House was new, and relatively unknown, very few people used it during the day. It would provide the kind of privacy a young skater needs when just starting out.

As Edward Van Campen, a figure skating coach at the Ice House, told the *New York Times*, "At the beginning…it was just the three of us on the ice — Sarah, Robin, and me."

(That would later change, after Craig Maurizi, the rink's figure skating director, coached Tara Lipinski to the Olympic gold medal in 1998. With Lipinski's success, top American and Russian coaches chose the Ice House as their primary training facility.)

But when Wagner first investigated the Ice

House as a possible place to train Sarah for an international career, it seemed perfect — lots of space, lots of time available, few skaters on the ice at any one time. There was only one problem with the Ice House. It was in Hackensack.

With the traffic, it could take anywhere from forty-five minutes up to two hours to drive there from Sarah's home in King's Point. Since Sarah would be increasing her practice schedule to 2½ or 3 hours per session, six days a week, that meant a daily commute that on the best days would take an hour and a half, and, if traffic were a problem, on the worst days would keep them in the car for four hours of roundtrip travel.

Conventional skating wisdom holds that a skater doesn't need long commutes; a skater doesn't need the distractions of family; a skater, even if she or he is a preteen, if they're serious about becoming an international champion, must leave home and move closer to their practice facility.

Once again, Robin Wagner, with the support and urging of John and Amy Hughes, bucked conventional wisdom. Wagner supported the Hughes' desire to provide Sarah a stable home life, to keep her a part of the family on a daily basis.

This meant that Sarah and Robin had to commute to the skating facility six days a week. Sarah's Mom would drop her off to Wagner at the parking lot in a local shopping mall six days a week, then pick her up when the skaters returned.

Wagner never complained, never suggested Sarah leave her home, move closer to the rink. Further, the coach set ground rules for the commute. They could talk about anything except skating. They listened to CDs — Sarah's favorites include Britney Spears, Celine Dion, the Backstreet Boys — talked about boys, make-up, movies, school.

♔

Robin Wagner soon became more than a coach. She became someone Sarah could trust and confide in, someone with whom she could laugh or cry. Sarah told Wagner all her fears and hopes and dreams. Her coach listened to her student, encouraged her, but gently made sure her goals were realistic.

Robin Wagner became someone Sarah could hang out with in the down time between competitions, go shopping with, or see a movie.

She became Sarah's friend, mentor, and surrogate mother.

Amy and John Hughes, wanting only the best for their daughter, knew they had found the perfect coach for Sarah. Robin Wagner was someone who could help Sarah fight for her dreams, but someone who could also help Sarah keep it all in perspective if those dreams, like John's dreams of becoming a professional hockey player, didn't turn out quite the way Sarah hoped they would.

These qualities in Robin Wagner were just as important to the Hughes' as her skating knowledge. And while others might have questioned Wagner's ability to coach a top talent, the Hughes family did not.

As a former skater who had never won a championship, Wagner knew what the difference was between those who won, and those who lost. She knew the importance of the grace and flow only a dance background could teach a skater. She knew Sarah's training in ballet would prove to be of great benefit in competition.

So Wagner, aware of the necessity to develop Sarah's artistic as well as technical side, appreciated Senn's work with the girl. Senn had given

Sarah a style of presentation that could be incorporated into the girl's routines. The basics were already in place. It was up to Wagner to help Sarah bring out the more creative part of her talent.

♛

But Wagner also knew that it wasn't only about artistic presentation. She knew that Sarah had to improve the technical aspects of her skating, too. When she began working with Sarah in 1995, Wagner undertook the long, arduous process of integrating art and technique that would bring Sarah, six years later, to center ice of the Delta Rink in Salt Lake City, and a fight for the Olympic gold medal.

These six years would be ones of grueling labor, intense focus, dedication, development, disappointment, and finally, triumph.

Chapter 6

To begin with, just to learn how to master the double axel, a basic move all skaters must learn before they can move on to the more complicated moves like the triple jumps that soon became Sarah's signature skill, takes a long time. It took Sarah two years of practice before she had her double axels down pat.

But Coach Wagner had to focus on more than just one move at a time. And competitive skating isn't only about technique.

During this time of learning the technical aspects of skating and performance, Robin Wagner worked hard with Sarah to implement an ambitious plan that would give Sarah experience in competition settings, while building her confidence.

She wanted Sarah to set achievable goals, but she also knew Sarah had to test herself against other skaters. So in 1996, when Sarah was still ten, Wagner took her to compete in the 1996 North

Sarah stretches out before practicing her long program at the Salt Lake Ice Center during the Winter Olympics in Salt Lake City on Feb 17, 2002.

Atlantic Regional Novice Championship, held that year in Canada. It was Sarah's first major qualifying competition. As was almost always the case, Sarah's family went with her, to give her support and encouragement.

Sarah, much to the delight of herself and her coach, finished third. At only ten years old, and in her first competition, she finished third. That placement qualified her to compete in the Eastern Sectional Novice Competition.

Although she claimed not to be expecting too much, after finishing third in her first ever competition there was a part of Sarah that thought maybe this was easier than she had been led to believe.

At the Eastern Sectionals, Sarah was given a stark reminder of how far she still had to go. She finished a distant tenth, too far back to even be considered for the National Novice Competition.

It was her first taste of competitive skating; her first success, and her first real disappointment. She realized she was no longer skating for a supportive audience of family and friends. Now, there were judges she had to impress.

Rather than brood on her disappointment, Sarah

and Robin took this as an opportunity to focus on what Sarah needed to do better for the next year. Under Wagner's tutelage, the young skater spent the following year refining her spins, jumps, glides, and twirls. She worked harder on her presentation. When she returned to compete in the 1997 North Atlantic Regional Novice Championship, she was ready. This time, Sarah won the gold medal.

At the Eastern Sectionals, Sarah improved dramatically over the year before. Still, the level of competition at the Easterns was higher. Only skaters who had won medals in previous juried competitions, as Sarah had at the North Atlantics, were invited to participate.

Although she improved over her previous year's performance, Sarah only came in sixth. Once again, she had failed to earn a spot at the National Competition.

Wagner emphasized the positive — the gold medal, the improvement Sarah had made at the Easterns. Sarah had accomplished what her coach had wanted to at that level. Coach and skater decided there was no sense staying in the Novice division any longer.

Having won the North Atlantic Novice

Nationals, Sarah was now eligible to move up in rank, to the next level, the Junior level. This was the only level Sarah still had to master before she could compete as a Senior skater. Sarah knew you had to be on the Senior level to qualify for the most prestigious competitions — the Senior Nationals, the World Championships, the Olympics.

Everything seemed to be moving, changing, so fast. She was moving up to another level of competition, the second highest level a skater could attain. This was probably going to be the hardest thing she'd dealt with so far, Sarah certainly thought to herself as she contemplated it all. Nothing in her life so far had been this difficult, this loaded with pressure.

But she was soon to learn the pressure of moving up a level in ice-skating wasn't anywhere near as difficult to deal with as the pressure of having to deal with the crisis that was about to strike her family.

Chapter 7

It started with a small lump. But even before Amy Hughes went to the doctor to get it checked out, she knew. The doctor's diagnosis confirmed her fears; Amy Hughes had breast cancer. No matter how good a face she tried to put on it, how hard she tried to play it down, remain upbeat about her prognosis for recovery, the family was devastated.

But the Hughes' were fighters, too, Amy no less than any of them. No one was willing to concede anything. Amy was not going to give up without a battle. Her family rallied around her.

What could a twelve-year-old girl do, though, to help her mother battle cancer? Sarah knew a little bit about cancer. Scott Hamilton, the champion

Sarah competes in the women's free skating program at the
Winter Olympic on February 21, 2002.

skater, had been diagnosed with testicular cancer.
He had beaten it.

Although there was no way to be certain, Sarah
was positive her mother could beat it, too. At least,

that was the public face Sarah put on, one of confidence.

But the public face of a twelve-year-old girl, when facing the very real threat that her mother

Another lyrical moment during Sarah's free skate program.

might die, sometimes masks the girl's true feelings. Public confidence often hides inner fears, especially when one feels helpless, unable to attack the source of those fears head on. It's not as if Sarah could go into her mother's body and pull out the cancer cells on with her own hands.

Sarah could have withdrawn into her own fear and heartbreak. She could've given up everything to spend all her time at home. And who would have criticized her for reacting in those ways? But she put on a brave face, told her mother she was confident she would survive. She told her mother she had no doubt about that. Since she couldn't go into her mother's body, fight the cancer herself, Sarah did the one thing she could do to help.

She skated.

As John Hughes told the *Great Neck Record*, for the first time, "She took ownership of her own skating.. . . She had to get herself up to go to practices, figure out how to get to and from the rink, learn her music, choose her costumes, everything. The competitions are maybe three percent of the process. She had to take it on herself."

Sarah determined that she would push forward

with everything she had. If her mother were going to die, she would die seeing her daughter use every ounce of talent God had given her. Sarah's skating would become part of her mother's cancer treatment.

"Her mother dubbed her Dr. Sarah," Rena Kunis wrote in the *Record*. "Watching her daughter skate eased Amy's mind and body from the rigors of cancer therapies."

Suddenly, finishing sixth didn't seem such a big deal anymore. Falling on the ice during a routine? How bad was that? Faced with the real problem of life and death, Sarah could put her skating in a proper perspective. Why hold back? Why play it safe? Why not risk being the best you could be on the ice? In human terms, that really wasn't much to risk to begin with. It was only ice skating, after all. And why wait to do it later? How much time was a person guaranteed in their life, anyway?

Wagner and Hughes trained hard, harder than ever before. The training certainly was a way for Sarah to lose herself. It gave her something to concentrate on so she wouldn't have to focus on the cancerous cells

Sarah is hugged by her coach Robin Wagner after her performance in the free skating program at the Winter Olympics February 21, 2002. Hughes won the gold medal in the event.

trying to destroy her mother. She could put all her energy on learning what she had to do — double axels, triple loops, spirals. There was so much to work on, and Sarah wanted to get it right. Judges had told Wagner after previous competitions that Hughes was weak in a couple of areas. She wasn't as artistically expressive as she needed to be. She also had trouble with her Lutz jump. They focused on those two areas.

And they also focused on triple jumps.

In the 1990s, as 'amateur' skaters spent more and more time training, and developed their technical skills to higher levels, triple jumps had become a more important part of a skater's repertoire. Tara Lipinski had landed two triple-triple combinations in her long program, and that was what won her the gold over the favored Michelle Kwan.

Sarah was a strong skater. Wagner knew she had the physical skills to compete with anyone. There was no reason she couldn't learn how to do triple jumps. It was all a matter of practice. Three hours a day, six days a week, every week of every month. Practice, repeat, refine. Wagner zeroed in on Sarah's technique, on her artistry, on her presentation, on integrating all the elements.

Although Sarah would be the youngest skater in her competitions, she needed to show the same level of maturity and sophistication as the older girls. Sarah didn't want to come across as a little girl among blossoming women.

Ironically, just as Sarah's skating would help her mother deal with having cancer, her mother's cancer, in a way, helped Sarah with her skating. When faced with a serious illness afflicting a parent, a child has to grow up immediately. The sudden need for Sarah to act with increased maturity at home, helped her mature on the ice.

Wagner worked hard with Sarah to integrate her athleticism with her background in ballet, to develop a style that would offer both technical dazzle and grace, that would show the judges Sarah was a young woman, no longer a girl.

In the fall of 1998, Sarah entered the North Atlantic Junior Regionals. She knew her mother would be following the competition. She knew how much it meant to her mother, how it kept her mother's mind off the own cancer treatments, if only for a brief time. Sarah took the ice determined to do what was in her power — to help her mother find something to celebrate, if only for a moment.

Sarah, the newer, more mature Sarah, won the first place gold medal.

She moved on to the Eastern Junior Sectionals.

As a novice, the Easterns had always given Sarah trouble in the past. But this was a new Sarah. Again, just as at the North Atlantic Competition, there was that same intensity, that same determination to skate her best, not just for herself this time, not just for the attention it would bring her, but to help her mother. It was the one thing, the only thing, a twelve-year-old girl could do.

Sarah won the first place gold at the 1998 Eastern Junior Regionals, too.

Now she was headed to Philadelphia, for the 1998 National Junior Championships. This was the first time Sarah had ever made it to the Nationals. Everyone in the Hughes family was ecstatic.

But there was a sorrow to Sarah's triumph, too. She would be the only skater who had to perform without her mother in the stands to cheer her on. For Amy Hughes was still undergoing chemotherapy. It left her too sick, too weak, to travel to watch her daughter compete.

Sarah's father would be there, as would her brothers and sisters. But as Sarah headed to Philadelphia for the biggest event of her young career, her mother stayed back home in a hospital bed, unable to move.

Until…until…it was time for the long program. Somehow, Amy Hughes got herself up out of her hospital bed and traveled to Philadelphia in time to sit with her family and watch her daughter compete. Inspired by her mother's courage, Sarah went out and skated the best program of her life. She won the first place gold.

At age twelve, Sarah Hughes was the 1998 U.S. Junior Ladies Champion.

The feat was applauded in *International Figure Skating*. The editors spoke of how the first place finish "confirmed what her friends and family have known for a long time — that her hard work and love for skating could translate into medals."

But perhaps they should've mentioned something else, too. Perhaps they should have mentioned something about how the power of love between a mother and daughter can create miracles on and off the ice.

Soon Amy's chemotherapy would end, and all

Sarah holds an American flag after performing in the 2002 Winter Olympic figure skating exhibition at the Salt Lake Ice Center in Salt Lake City, February 22,2002.

traces of the cancer would disappear. She could return to her old life.

But for Sarah, there was no way to return to her old life. "Juniors is really just the beginning," Robin Wagner told *The Augusta Chronicle*. "Winning Juniors put her into the arena where she can really further her career."

The win at Nationals had vaulted Sarah into a new place in the skating world, an exhilarating and terrifying place from which there was no turning back. A place where some skaters learned to soar, and others were destroyed forever.

Chapter 8

The year she turned thirteen, the year she won the first place gold at the National Junior Championships, the United States Figure Skating Association asked Sarah Hughes to participate in the Junior Grand Prix circuit.

The circuit is a series of international competitions where skaters from all over the world compete in different events. The medal winners at each event collect points. At the end of the circuit, the six skaters with the most points are invited to compete at the Junior Grand Prix Final.

The first competition, for the Hungary Trophy, was held in Budapest, Hungary, in November. It would be broadcast on ESPN. Sarah, a girl who had always enjoyed the limelight, would now be seen by perhaps millions of people around the globe. Although her parents wouldn't be watching. At least, they wouldn't be watching on ESPN.

Now that Amy Hughes had finished her therapy, she was strong enough to travel. The family flew to Europe with Sarah, so they could all be together. They hung out together, did some sight seeing. Sarah even spent considerable time on her schoolwork.

On the ice, Sarah put on a strong performance. In her first competition in the Junior Grand Prix circuit, Sarah Hughes won the silver medal, second place, in Hungary.

From Europe, the competition moved to Mexico City. Again, her family flew with her. Again, Sarah finished second, winning the silver medal.

She had now earned enough points to qualify for the Junior Grand Prix final. That competition would be held in Detroit, Michigan in March of 1999. True to that year's form, Sarah finished second, winning yet another silver medal.

But before Sarah went to Detroit there was

The winners of the Olympic women's figure skating competition show off their medals. They are from left, Irina Slutskaya of Russia, silver; Sarah Hughes of the US., gold; and Michelle Kwan, US, bronze.

another, more important competition, she resolved to enter.

After consultations with her coach, Sarah decided, even though she might be the youngest one in the competition, it was now time for her to move up to the Senior level.

This was the year to do it, Sarah thought. She had proven she was one of the top Junior skaters. She had nothing to gain by staying at that level any longer. To move up to Seniors, she only needed to pass a skills test, which was no problem for her.

So Sarah and Robin prepared to skate in both the Junior Grand Prix final and, before that, the 1999 U.S. National Seniors Championship. It would be a good test for Sarah, they thought, to see how she'd skate against some of the top Seniors in the U.S. The competition would be a challenge, and so would the ice surface.

The Seniors Championship was to be held at a venue where Sarah had never skated before, the new Delta Center, in Salt Lake City. At that point in her career, it was the largest ice-skating rink Sarah had ever competed on.

There wouldn't be quite as much pressure on Sarah to perform, they believed. She was only thirteen, and both Robin and Sarah believed she was too young to be sent on to the World Championships, even if she medalled. Under international rules, a skater had to be at least fifteen years old to compete at the Worlds.

So, for Sarah, the Nationals competition didn't bear the weight of qualifying for the next event, the next rung in the Seniors skating ladder. Sarah could skate just to try things out, see how she fit with the older skaters. Sarah headed to Salt Lake City feeling relatively relaxed.

For most thirteen-year-old girls, being at the U.S. Senior National Championships would be intimidating. But Sarah wasn't like most thirteen-year-old girls. "My problems," Amy Hughes told *The Daily News*, "put everything in perspective (for her)."

That doesn't mean Sarah took her good fortune lightly, though. She was excited to be on the same ice as many of the top U.S. skaters.

"I think every girl who goes to Seniors for the first time walks in the dressing room and thinks, 'Oh my God! There's Michelle Kwan!'" Sarah told a press conference. "My problem was that I almost blurted out, 'Oh my God! There's Michelle Kwan!'"

Sitting at the press table, Sarah glanced over at Michelle. "It seems like a dream," Sarah said. "I can't believe I'm sitting next to her."

But anyone who thought Sarah was just some goggle-eyed youngster would be underestimating her inner drive.

And while some might've dismissed her as a fluke, others in attendance knew. The Editor of

International Figure Skating, Lois Elfman, had scrutinized all the girls who were competing. "I had seen Sarah skate, and I thought she could do really well."

Sarah Hughes did not make a single mistake in her short program, the program where there are specific elements all skaters have to attempt. Her flawless performance put her in second place in the standings going into the long program. In first place was her idol, Michelle Kwan.

Sarah took the ice first in her group of six, with Michelle waiting to follow. As the music to 'Swan Lake' filtered around her, Sarah attempted her first jump of the program.

And she fell.

She told herself it was okay, she had to get up, she had to go on, don't panic. She righted herself, resumed her routine, and quickly launched into a triple lutz. The landing was flawless. She seemed to be back in control of the program. Maybe a medal wasn't out of the realm of possibility after all.

But as Sarah set up for a combination, she stumbled and fell once more.

Once again she had to get quickly to her feet without losing focus. This time she threw herself into a triple loop-triple loop combination, and nailed it.

When she finished her routine, she knew. "I thought I performed okay," she said, trying to mask her disappointment. She took comfort from the fact that this was the first time she had ever performed at the Nationals. It was a big step for her, just to be there.

As it was, Sarah finished in fourth, certainly nothing to be ashamed of. The third place finisher was another thirteen year old girl, Naomi Nari Nam. Third and fourth for two thirteen-year-olds – well, that was a good showing for the younger kids.

As Sarah prepared to go home, assuming the committee would pick an older skater to accompany Michelle Kwan and Angela Nikodinov, the first and second place winners, to the World Championships, Sarah was told to get her bags packed — for Helsinki, the World Championships.

♆

Sarah and her coach had been right about international rules requiring all senior skaters to be fifteen years old. But they had both overlooked a minor portion of the rules. True, a skater could only compete in the World Championships if they were fifteen years old.

Unless…unless they had earned a medal from that year's Junior World Championship.

Sarah, of course, had won the silver. Despite her age, under international rules, Sarah could compete against the best Senior skaters. Sarah Hughes, just thirteen, was going to her first World Championship.

Chapter 9

I know she's good, but she's only thirteen," Amy Hughes told the *Great Neck Record* when asked how she felt about her daughter being selected to represent the United States at the 1999 Worlds Championship.

Sarah had a somewhat different take on the age question. "It's cool," she told a press conference, sounding as perky and giggly as a young adolescent girl.

In the short program, she skated a bit like a young girl awed by the competition. Her movements were tighter than normal, lacked their usual flowing grace. She was in ninth place entering the long program.

But Sarah wasn't content to be treated like the cute little girl invited to the big girls' party.

Later, in a TV interview with Leslie Visser, Sarah revealed her true feelings. She had an agenda at the Worlds. She wanted to "Show that thirteen-year-olds can come and look like they belong."

That was a point her coach Robin Wagner reiterated to Sarah as they prepared to skate — she did belong. She had earned the right to be there. She was good enough to compete.

Sarah made no mistakes in her long program. She landed all her jumps, including a triple lutz. "I was pretty nervous today," she said as she left the ice. "I'm just happy I skated as well as I did."

She skated well enough to finish in seventh place, one place higher than Michelle Kwan had finished in her first Worlds. Sarah was now ranked as one of the top ten skaters in the world.

The speed with which Sarah Hughes had climbed from novice skater to a competitor at the World Championships was phenomenal. Not only had she risen three levels in her skating, she had grown up as a person, too.

"When I was a novice skater, she (Michelle Kwan) was the American champion and she was winning a lot of competitions," Hughes told the *New York Times*. "It was natural for me to look up to her, to root for her, to cheer for her. But now...." Hughes said, "She's just another competitor. Everybody is another competitor."

The young skater felt she was ready to assume her place among the skating elite.

Chapter 10

In the fall of 1999 Sarah Hughes had many things to balance. She was starting high school, enrolled in honors classes. Opportunities to skate in various 1999-2000 Senior events were coming in so fast, it soon became apparent there wasn't time to commit to all of them. Robin Wagner sat down with her star skater and they planned out a schedule that would allow Sarah to grow and develop, while also testing herself against strong competition. And Sarah's family helped by lining up tutors to work with their daughter on her schoolwork.

Sarah began her season with a competition in Canada, then flew to Florida, moved on to Vienna, where Sarah, for the first time that season, won an individual first place award. More importantly, after attending a performance of Puccini's opera *Turandot*, Robin and Sarah discovered, in the opera, a story and music that would work well with the interpretive skating — skating that relies less on technical brilliance and more on expressing, through movement, the emotions of a piece of music — Sarah was working hard to master.

Sarah hurried to prepare her *Turandot* piece for the Skate America competition, her first stop on the Senior Grand Prix circuit. She spent a lot of time working, like a dancer, in front of mirrors. On the ice, she was trying to develop all the small details of transition, the "in-betweens" as she called them.

It takes time to work with a new piece of music, though. When it came time for the competition to begin, Sarah hadn't fully mastered her new routine. Yet she still finished fourth, three spots behind Michelle Kwan.

At the Trophy Lalique in Paris, Sarah's second Grand Prix event, she moved up to third, Sarah's first medal on the Senior tour. When asked at a press conference if she felt intimidated at having to skate against World Champion Maria Butyrskaya, who won the event, Sarah told the interviewer:

"Not at all, it's an honor to skate with her because she is the World Champion and I respect World Champions."

But she wasn't in awe of them either. She didn't consider then to be better than herself. Sarah added, "We all respect each other."

Her year of practice and hard work had prepared Sarah well to compete for the 2000 United States Nationals Championship.

Throughout the year, she had worked hard on learning how to interpret music through gestures and movements. She had refined her presentation to develop dancer-like lines, grace and flow. She had pushed herself to master difficult technical moves, like triple jumps. Sarah was growing into a Senior skater. She felt ready.

In the short program, Sarah's skating displayed her confidence. She finished second, sandwiched between Sasha Cohen, in third, and Michelle Kwan, in first place.

For the long program, Sarah was slotted to skate first in her group of six. She burst onto the ice, stunning the crowd early with a triple salchow-triple loop. No female skater, including Sarah, had ever landed that triple-triple combination in competition.

She was skating strongly, the crowd behind her, until, during an attempt to land a triple salchow, it happened again.

She fell.

Sarah finished third, behind Kwan and Cohen. Still, that medal earned her a spot on the U.S. team that would be traveling to France for the 2000 World Championships. She didn't make it on a legal ruling this time. She belonged on the basis of her own performance.

But there was one more thing Sarah needed to do before competing at the Worlds. She decided it was time to chop off her long, girlish ponytail in favor of the type of short, cropped-back style in vogue with women in their early twenties.

This was as much a statement as it would have been had Sarah stood at a microphone and told the judges, "Don't treat me like a little girl anymore."

Chapter 11

At the 2000 World Championships, Sarah shocked everyone by how well she skated in the qualifying round, which would enable her to skate in the competition round. Her improvement over her skating at the Nationals was dramatic. Skating in a group of experienced medal winners, Sarah finished third, behind Russia's Irina Slutskaya and Michelle Kwan.

The editor of *International Figure Skating*, Lois Elfman, said, "Sarah had improved every element of her skating. Everything . . . she had made one hundred percent the transition to Senior. Tremendous progress from girl to woman."

Sarah skated well in the competition, though not

flawlessly. She finished in fifth place. At the young age of fourteen, she was considered the fifth best skater in the world.

Sarah returned home for the summer and devised a plan with her coach that would take her to the next level. They would spend the summer trying to master a triple axel, the jump that is generally considered the most difficult in women's figure skating.

But on the first day of training Sarah broke her hand when she slammed into the boards. Then, she overdid her aerobic exercises and injured her hip muscle.

♆

The now fifteen-year-old girl had nothing to do for the next two months but sit around the house. As if that weren't bad enough, Sarah grew another couple of inches, so her height reached five feet four and a half inches, which was very tall for a skater. And sitting around the house, with nothing to do, she began to put on weight. Sarah grew more and more depressed.

The beginning of the skating season was not far off and Sarah was in no way prepared for it. Robin Wagner took control of her pupil. She put her on a strict diet and challenged her to get up, get busy, and show people what kind of skating she could really do.

Sarah responded to the challenge. At Skate America, her first Grand Prix event, Sarah finished second. At the Cup of Russia competition, she finished third. In Germany, at the Nations Cup, only former World Champion Maria Butyrskaya was good enough to beat her. And at the Grand Prix Final, Sarah finished third, knocking Butyrskaya into fourth place.

Sarah told the Associated Press, "It's probably the best four weeks of my life."

At the 2001 National Championships, Sarah skated to a silver medal. Only Michelle Kwan scored higher.

Sarah told the *New York Times* that she had learned a lot, sitting home when she was injured. "Things don't always go as planned." So it became more important than ever for Sarah to embrace the opportunities that came her way.

She headed to Canada for the World

Championships. Skating to *Don Quixote*, Sarah pulled out all the stops. Triple salchows, triple loops, triple lutz, triple toe, combinations, spins. She also "played" the judges in a way she never had before, smiling, flirting, acting sexy. When she finished she was so excited she pumped her fist in the air and clapped for herself.

The scores came in. Sarah Hughes, for the first time, received higher grades for her artistic presentation than for her technical skating. Presentation had finally caught up with technique. In only her third appearance at the World Championships, Sarah won the bronze medal.

Her road to the Olympics continued throughout 2001. A second place finish at Skate America, second at Trophee Lalique, first at Skate Canada. In early 2002, she finished third, behind Michelle Kwan and Sasha Cohen, at the U.S. Nationals.

Sarah Hughes, just sixteen years old, would be representing the United States at the Olympic games.

And as everyone was sure to find out, Sarah wasn't content merely to be *going* to the Olympics. She was going to the Olympics to try to win.

Chapter 12

Sarah Hughes drifted to her starting position on the ice in the Delta Center rink for the start of her long program, her final performance at the 2002 Winter Olympics. As she struck her initial pose, and waited for the first strains of her opening music to filter through the air, she certainly must've felt the restraint in the crowd. Yes, there was energy — this was the Olympics, after all — but it was subdued, held back in wait for the real contenders, as if the majority of those in the crowd were assured this would be a preliminary to the main competition.

But then something happened. As Sarah began her routine the crowd perked up, the energy began to slowly increase in intensity. Sarah was skating well. In fact, she was skating flawlessly.

Her coach, Robin Wagner, knew they had a chance. "Sarah is better as the chaser, than as the one being chased," she later told *Newsweek*. Those who had dismissed Sarah underestimated this winsome teenager's determination. And they had forgotten that Sarah was a great skater. She was elegant, focused, rarely made mistakes on the ice, and was capable of strong jumps and triple-triple combinations. She had beaten Kwan and Slutskaya and Cohen in other international competitions. These facts, the fickle skating fans and media seemed to have forgotten.

Later Sarah would say, "I had nothing to lose." There were no expectations on her, so she could let it all hang out. The first part of this special day had been normal enough. There was morning practice, lunch, a short walk, a nap, a snack ordered from room service; skater and coach didn't even get to the rink until 7:30.

Seemingly freed from all pressure, now Sarah focused into a Zen-like state. She became one with her skates, the ice, the audience. It soon became apparent something rare and wonderful was happening at Delta Center. People began to realize how good a skater Sarah was. The people in the audience sat straighter in their seats, began to concentrate harder. When she launched — and nailed — her first triple-triple combination, the audience responded with screams and applause. The energy bumped up a notch. On the ice, she could feel it, almost like a spiritual force, feeding her without distracting her attention.

When Sarah completed her second triple-triple jump, she herself clapped her hands and screeched with delight. The crowd erupted in a frenzy. They cheered every jump and twirl, every gliding stride across the ice. They roared their approval louder and louder. The energy soared higher and Sarah became one with the energy, too. She wasn't performing any longer; she *was* the skating, at one with the moment.

By the time she completed her routine, the spectators in the stands all knew. Even before the judges announced the scores, they knew. Even more than Sarah, the people in the arena knew that had just witnessed something rare and marvelous. Seven triple jumps, two triple-triple combinations, in a flawlessly skated performance of elegance and grace.

As reported by *Newsweek* magazine, when Sarah skated off the ice, Coach Wagner "seized her by the shoulders" and made her face the crowd. "I said to her, 'Just turn around. Close your eyes. Take a deep breath. Now open your eyes. I want you to remember this moment forever.'"

Sarah turned to see a riotous standing ovation, so many flowers floating down through the air it was as if heaven were raining petals onto the Delta Center ice.

The scores came out and they were outstanding — except for those of the Russian and Danish judges, who would be the only two judges to list Sarah fourth in their final tallies. But that wasn't the end of it. The three top-seeded skaters still had to perform. If only one of them skated up to their potential, Sarah would lose any chance she had at a gold. If all three skated well, Sarah wouldn't even make it onto the stage for the medals ceremony.

Hughes and Wagner settled onto a hard bench in a backstage room. The space was bare, devoid of light and energy, bleak in comparison to the expansive rink where Hughes had just skated, with its tiered seats and screaming crowd. Sarah sat there, a child, a 16-year-old girl, waiting nervously with her coach, this woman who had been a surrogate mother these past six years.

They waited in that strange moral universe of competitive athletics, where you do and you don't wish your rivals well — your rivals, other girls just like you, girls who have experimented with make-up and giggled over cute boys just like you, girls who had dreamed since childhood of being that smiling princess who stands on the Olympic reviewing stand to receive a medal — just like you. You wait and you hope that they fail, they mess up, they make a mistake that will insure your own victory. You hope for this even as you feel bad for wishing ill luck on another girl. But you want to win. You want to win so badly.

♀

First came Sasha Cohen, the new teenaged darling. Cohen began with predictable élan, displaying the sharp lines and dramatic style that leaves audiences breathless with delight.

But something unexpected happened. Cohen faltered. She slumped at the end of a combination jump, failing to land it cleanly. She seemed momentarily uncertain, and the crowd sensed it, their enthusiasm held back. Although she would pull it together, and go on to finish strongly, it was too late. She had made a fatal mistake. Cohen skated off, knowing she had failed to take advantage of her opportunity.

Michelle Kwan skated next. The much-loved veteran had been defeated at the previous Olympics by Tara Lipinski. Never the most energetic skater, Kwan had earned her awards by virtue of the superior grace and beauty of her skating.

Perhaps after witnessing Hughes' performance, the memory of Kwan's earlier Olympic failure haunted her. She was obviously nervous, seemed to lack her usual confidence. She gave up on her triple-triple jump and settled for a triple-double. The failure to follow through, to settle for a triple-double, was like admitting she had no chance. It sucked the energy out of her. Later, on a triple flip, a routine maneuver, Michelle Kwan fell, ending her dreams of winning an Olympic gold medal.

Finally it was time for Slutskaya, the most physical of all the skaters, a woman noted for her powerful leaps, her ability to nail triple-triple jumps with precision. Slutskaya was generally conceded to be the strongest skater in the competition. In the past, though, she lacked the delicate artistry of her rivals. One pundit compared her to a hockey player crashing into the corner for the puck.

Still, it seemed the gold was hers for the taking. All she needed to do was skate one of her typically strong routines.

But something went awry. Although she made no mistakes, neither stumbled nor fell, Slutskaya didn't attempt a single triple-triple combination. Her program, usually energetic, seemed almost lazy, lethargic. She wasted valuable time merely standing before the judges, winding her arms in slow, sinuous movements. Perhaps she had antic-ipated that her main competition would by Kwan, and so had devised a routine that would attempt to beat Kwan at her own game; gracefulness, delicacy, poise.

In a way, it worked. Slutskaya did beat Kwan. Even the American judge rated Irina's performance more highly than Kwan's. But in defeating Kwan, all Slutskaya accomplished was preventing Kwan from achieving the gold medal. Because if Irina had finished *behind* Kwan, because of Kwan's first place ranking in the short program, Kwan would've edged out Hughes for the gold medal.

Slutskaya had failed to compete against the skater who had the strongest performance of the night – Sarah Hughes.

And the combination of her own great performance, plus the scoring protocal, had enabled this sixteen-year-old high school junior from Kings Point New Jersey who had been given no chance, no chance at all to win a gold medal, to pull off one of the biggest upsets in Olympic history. This was the type of dream achievement you expect to see in a Walt Disney movie, but here it was, as real as the ice at Delta Center in Salt Lake City.

How many grade B movies center on the underdog winning against all odds? If this were to be made into a film, it might be titled "The Accidental Champion."

But that would not be true. The title would be a lie.

There was nothing accidental about Sarah Hughes' success. The gold medal she earned was the culmination of thirteen years of grueling labor, practice, dedication, and commitment to a dream.

She had started as a small child, perhaps to gain her parents' approval, perhaps to set herself a bit apat in a close but highly competitive, high-achieving family. And now, a lifetime later (perhaps one could say, a *short* lifetime), she was briefly at the center of the world, a media darling, a world champion.

It seemed such a long time, but such a short time, too.

And her life as an Olympic champion was really just beginning.

Chapter 13

I enjoy being the center of attention," Sarah told *Cleveland.com*. She enjoys it when reporters follow her around at school. She likes sitting at the press table at skating events, talking about her experiences on the ice. She gets excited when she's on TV and others can see her. She's thrilled when her family decorates the house to show their support for her, when everyone travels to see her skate. She loves seeing posters in the windows of the shops in her hometown.

After the Olympics, Sarah received more attention than she had ever dreamed of. She rang the opening bell on Wall Street; she was a presenter, with the Backstreet Boys, at the Grammy Awards. She was courted by every TV and radio talk show, every newspaper in the country, all wanting a piece of her, all wanting to give her attention. Her hometown gave her a parade, at which tens of thousands of people lined the streets waving and screaming of their love for Sarah Hughes, Olympic gold medallist.

On a some what different note, Sarah's gold medal performance was given an honor accorded to only a few previews athletes. Her image was featured on a special-edition package of Wheaties brand cereal. Previously honored athletes include gymnast Mary Lou Retton and speed skating Olympian Eric Heiden.

⟊

So, it has been a long ride in terms of distance but also a very fast one in terms of time. But what happens next? How long can Sarah ride this wave of success? Or perhaps, how long will she care to? What happens the first time she appears at a competition and she comes in second, or third?

What happens when she finishes out of the running for a medal? What happens when some new teenaged phenom bursts onto the international ice skating stage and wins over the judges' hearts?

Will it be enough for Sarah to do "Holiday On Ice" -type skating shows with Michelle Kwan and Sasha Cohen? Can she settle for half-attentive audiences in arenas in small cities like Madison, Wisconsin, and Nashville, Tennessee, stands full of people who will applaud inbetween eating their popcorn and taking their toddlers to the bathroom? Will that be enough for Sarah Hughes, this aggressively talented girl, who as a three-year-old, streaked onto the ice with an intensity that seemed to cry out 'Look at me! Look at me!'

As a skater, Sarah won the gold medal after she learned how to stop being a cute little girl with loads of talent, and to become a woman. She learned a more complex way of making people pay attention to her.

As an adult, will she find a more mature way to

get the attention she needs, and give something back to those who look to her?

No one knows for sure.

But would you bet against her?

Appendix 1

For the Record . . .

(Competitions and Place Finishings)

2002 International Olympics, 1st
2002 US Nationals Championships, 3rd
2002 Grand Prix Final, 3rd

2001 Hershey's Kisses Challenge (team) 2nd;
(individual) 4th
2001 Trophee Lalique, 2nd
2001 Skate Canada, 1st
2001 Skate America, 2nd
2001 Great American Figure Skating Challenge
(team), 3rd
2001 World Championships, 3rd
2001 Grand Prix Final, 3rd
2001 US National Championships, 2nd

2000 Canadian Open, 3rd

2000 Hershey's Kisses Challenge (individual) 1st; (team) 1st

2000 Cup of Russia, 3rd

2000 Nations Cup, 2nd

2000 Skate America, 2nd

2000 International Figure Skating Challenge (individual); 2nd (team) 2nd

2000 World Championships, 5th

2000 US Nationals, 3rd

1999 USA v. The World Pro Am (individual) 1st (team) 1st

1999 Trophy Lalique, 3rd

1999 Skate America, 4th

1999 Vienna Cup (Karl Schafer Memorial), 1st

1999 Keri Lotion Classic (individual.) 6th; (team) 2nd

1999 Grand Slam of Skating (pair--with Yevgeni Plushenko)(pair) 1st; (individual.) 4th

1999 Hershey's Kisses Figure Skating Challenge (Team USA): Sarah won her individual match-up against Katarina Witt, 2nd

1999 World Championships, 7th

1999 ISU Junior Grand Prix Final, 2nd

1999 U.S. Senior National Championships, 4th

1999 World Junior Championships, 2nd

1998 Hungary Trophy, 2nd

1999 World Junior Team Selection Competition, 1st

1998 Mexico Cup, 2nd

1998 National Junior Championships, 1st

1998 Eastern Junior, 1st

1998 North Atlantic Junior, 1st

1997 Eastern Novice, 6th

1997 North Atlantic Novice, 1st

1996 Eastern Novice, 10th

1996 North Atlantic Novice, 3rd

Appendix II

Skating Jumps

The six most common jumps that an ice skater uses in competition are, in descending order of difficulty, the axel, lutz, flip, loop, salchow, and toe.

These jumps are divided into two categories, *Edge* jumps and *Toe Pick Assisted* jumps.

The axel, loop, and salchow are *Edge* jumps.

The lutz, flip, and toe loop are *Toe Pick Assisted* jumps.

In *Edge* jumps a skater takes off from one foot. In *Toe Pick Assisted* jumps the skater uses the toe of the second foot to assist in leaping into the air.

The *axel* is considered the most difficult because it is the only jump where a skater takes off while moving forward, as opposed to being in a stationary position. On an axel, a skater takes off on the forward outside edge of her skate and lands on her opposite foot, this time on the back outside edge of the skate.

In a *loop*, the skater takes off and lands on the back outside edge of the same foot.

A *salchow* is similar to a loop with this exception: A skater takes off on the back inside edge of her skate and lands on the back outside edge of the same skate.

When performing a *lutz*, the skater takes off on the back outside edge of her skate and lands on the back outside edge of her opposite foot.

To perform a *flip,* a skater takes off on the back inside edge of her skate and lands on the back outside edge of her opposite foot.

A *toe loop* requires a dancer to take off and land on the back outside edge of the same skate.

Index

About the Author

RICHARD KRAWIEC lives in Raleigh, North Carolina with his family. He is Director of VOICES, a non-profit art organization working with, and publishing writing by, at-risk children and adults in homeless shelters, literacy classes, housing projects, and prisons. As a writer. he has won fellowships from the National Endowment for the Arts, The Pennsylvania Council on the Arts and the North Carolina Arts Council.